Beaded Lace
Snowflake Ornaments

Sandra D. Halpenny

Beaded Lace Snowflake Ornaments

Published by: Sandra D. Halpenny
Canadian Intellectual Property Office
Certificate of Copyright Registration #1070279

Beaded Lace Snowflake Ornaments
ISBN 978-0-9737973-6-7

Patterns tested by: Julia Wentz
Editor: Rosalie Wakefield

Every effort has been made to ensure that all the information in this book is accurate. However, due to differing conditions, tools and individual skills, the publisher cannot be responsible for any injuries, losses or other damages that may result from the use of the information in this book.

The finished items made from this book can be made for personal use and for individual's own pin money. You have my permission to make and sell at arts and craft shows, etc. No MASS production allowed. You may NOT teach classes from this book without written permission from the author.

http://www.SandraDHalpenny.com

TABLE OF CONTENTS

BEADS

All my patterns are designed using Miyuki® seed beads. I like to use the Japanese seed beads because they are uniform in size and the holes are large and even and wide enough to go through with thread several times.

Of course, you can use any kind of seed beads, but some of the patterns might need to be adjusted. Do a small section first to see how your seed beads will work.

THREAD

What you would look for is a beading thread with a weight of D. My favorites are Nymo and C-Lon thread. This is a thread that is not too heavy and not too thin. Match the color of thread to the color of beads that are in your project. I have recently started using Fireline® fishing line, too. I like 4lb and 6lb for bead weaving. You do not need to stretch or wax it.

Whether using thread or fishing line, for ease in threading the beading needle use a Sharpie marker and touch the tip of the thread. The marker makes the end of the thread more visible and it also stiffens the end of the thread so that it goes more easily into the needle hole.

SNOWFLAKE WEAVING TIPS

NEEDLES

Beading needles come in different lengths and sizes. You will need sizes #11 and #12 beading needles. They come in short and long versions. I use the John James sharps. I prefer the short, but it really makes no difference if you use either one.

BEESWAX

Beeswax is used for conditioning your thread. It can also help to keep your thread from tangling. You can get it from any beading store. Fabric stores also sell beeswax in a round plastic container.

SCISSORS

You will need a small, very sharp scissors. Invest in a good pair; it is worth it.

CLEAR NAIL POLISH

No, we are not going to do our nails. Nail polish is used for holding your knots and your thread in place. Only use fresh clear polish. Note: If you are using dyed beads, check for color fastness before using the polish. Sometimes polish removes color from the beads.

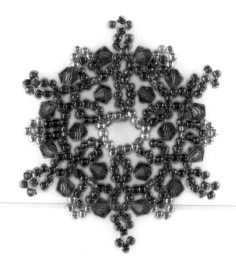

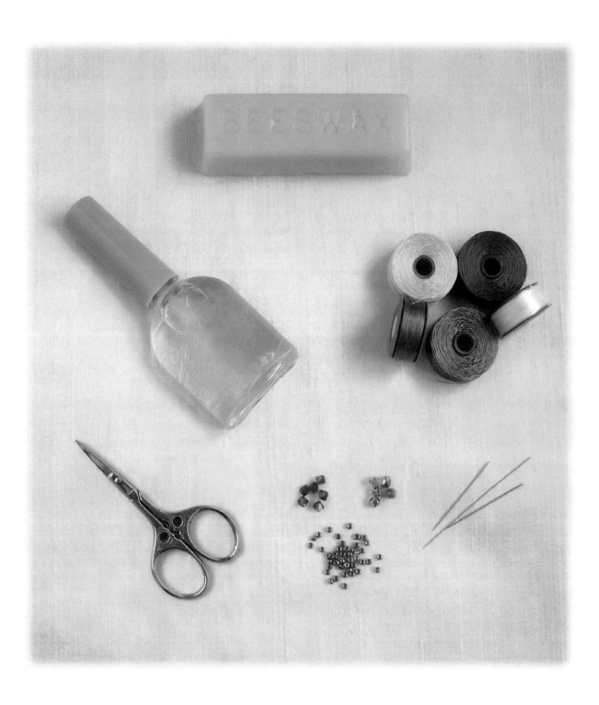

PORTABLE WORK AREA

This is how I move around the house with what I am working on.

I first start with a lap desk. This is a flat board, about 12" x 10", attached to a pillow. Cut a piece of no-slip vinyl shelf liner to fit (this keeps the tray in place, even if you have to get up really fast) and put that on the lap desk. Next, add a tray. You do not want the tray to have edges that are too high; otherwise, it will bother your arm if you are working on your lap.

Then add another piece of shelf liner and finally a placemat. I use a tightly-woven placemat, so the beads don't get lost in the texture of the fabric. It also keeps the beads from bouncing at you when you are working. If I am working at a table, I just use the tray part, but if I am working on my lap, I use the whole set up.

This is how I lay out my work surface. I bring the needle to the beads on the tray when picking up, not the beads to the needle. The little silver spoon I use for scooping up beads to put them away.

TERMINOLOGY

These are the terms that I use.

Each pattern tells you the type of beads that are used for the pattern.

W = Miyuki® 11/0 seed bead **C** = 4mm crystal AB

Pick up 4W, 1C, 3W

PICK UP
Pick up, is used for the amount and type of beads that you pick up on your working needle and thread. The picture above shows, Pick up 4A, 1B, 3A.

GO WITH THREAD
Go with thread refers to your working thread and needle.

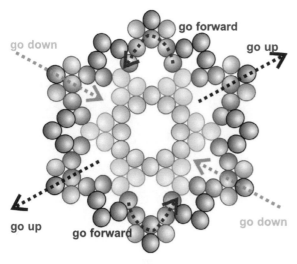

go down   go forward   go up

go up   go forward   go down

go forward
go up
go down

Go forward (counter-clockwise), is to go with your working thread and needle in the same direction as all the steps have gone. Go up, is to go toward the outside of the snowflake and go down, is to go down toward the center of the snowflake.

TO START

Cut about 1 yard of thread. When you get more experienced, you can start with a longer thread. When you cut the thread, cut it on an angle. This makes it easier to thread into the needle.

Run the thread through the beeswax a couple of times. Then run the thread through your fingers and stretch the thread as you are rubbing off the excess wax. DO NOT skip the stretching of the thread part. This is a big mistake that beginners make, including myself when I began. What can happen if you don't stretch the thread, after awhile the thread will start to stretch on it's own with the weight of the beads and the tension will become too loose. As you are working, keep in mind your tension. You don't want the tension too tight, but you also don't want to see the thread.
Please Note: If you are using fishing line, you do not need to wax or stretch it.

Thread your beading needle. Hint: Pinch the thread between your thumb and finger. Then bring the thread to the needle hole. Beading needle holes are very small, so it takes a bit of patience when you first start to thread them.

Now you need to add a stopper bead to the end of the working thread. I use an over hand knot, so the bead will hold, but will also slide off easily. This bead can be a different color. The stopper bead is used to hold your beads on while you work on your piece and helps to keep your tension.

Pick up the stopper bead, slide it down to the end of your working thread, leaving at least an 8" tail. With the thread, make a loop over your stopper bead bringing the left end thread over and through the back of the right hand thread. Pull up ends so the thread is snug around the stopper bead.

When you are done, you can pull off the stopper bead by putting the blunt end of your needle through the bead and pull it off by sliding down the thread tail.

BRINGING IN NEW THREAD,

AND ENDING THE OLD THREAD

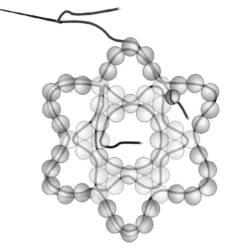

When you start to run out of thread or if you see that your working thread is starting to fray, it is time to bring a new thread in and end the old thread.

The light blue line in the diagram at right represents the finished working thread. Go with thread back though several beads in your bead weaving. Make a half hitch knot (shown in diagram as light blue dots). Weave through several more beads again with your working thread and make another half hitch knot, but before pulling up the thread to tighten the knot, put a bit of the clear nail polish on the knot area and about 1/4" along the thread. Pull up the knot tight and continue with the working thread through several more beads in your piece. Trim off the thread as close as possible to the beads.

Please note: If you make a knot, and you need to go through the bead where the knot is, the bead hole will be blocked. You can go back later to do the knotting. You never want to force the needle though beads, the beads are made of glass and can be broken.

The red line in the diagram represents bringing in a new thread with a stopper bead. The stopper bead can be removed after several steps have been completed in the pattern. Pull off the stopper bead and weave off the end of the new thread in the opposite direction of the old thread.

THE HALF HITCH KNOT

To make a half hitch knot, go around the thread in the piece with your working thread and needle between 2 beads. Make a loop and go through the loop in the working thread, pull up to tighten.
Please note: When weaving your threads through areas that already have been done, try not to split the threads with your working needle as it can weaken your threads.

BEAD COLORS FOR ROUNDS

R = Round

● Each Round begins at the red dot in diagram

Most of the snowflakes are done in Rounds. The Rounds are normally worked counter-clockwise unless otherwise noted.

Throughout this book the same colors are used for the Rounds as shown below.

W bead AB bead

◯	◯	Round 1
◯	◯	Round 2
◯	◯	Round 3
◯	◯	Round 4
◯	◯	Round 5
◯	◯	Round 6
◯	◯	Round 7

MAKING HANGERS FOR YOUR SNOWFLAKE

Using beads, make a loop with as many beads as you would like.

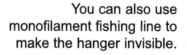

You can also use monofilament fishing line to make the hanger invisible.

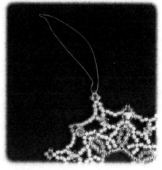

A piece of pretty ribbon also makes a very pretty hanger. Add ribbon after your snowflake is stiffened.

SNOWFLAKE FINISHING

After the snowflake is complete, you can stiffen it with *Pledge® with Future® Shine* (http://www.floorcareproducts.com/floor-finish/). It is a great stiffener and it stays clear, even on the crystals. Test it first if you use seed beads with dyed colors to make sure the floor finish doesn't remove the colors.

Pour enough of the Future Shine into a small container that is wide enough for the ornament. Float the ornament in the Future and push it around a bit with your finger. (After I am done with the Future Shine, I use a funnel and poor the extra back into the bottle)

Take the ornament out and blot both sides with a paper towel.

Put the ornament on a piece of wax paper, shape and flatten it and let it remain on the wax paper to dry. (If you use plastic wrap, the beads can stick a bit to the wrap, so it needs to be moved around a bit to prevent this from happening). If your ornament needs a little extra flattening, use two pieces of wax paper and sandwich your ornament in between; put a book on top of the wax paper for about an hour. Take the book and the top piece of wax paper off the ornament and let dry overnight on the bottom piece of wax paper.

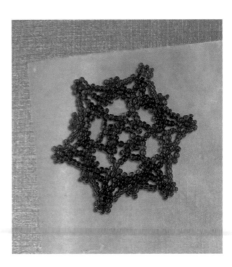

SNOWFLAKE ORNAMENT #1
2-1/4 INCHES

W = Miyuki® 11/0 seed bead, #528, All Rounds
C = 4mm crystal AB, R3

W = Miyuki® 11/0 seed bead, #25F, all Rounds
C = 4mm fire-polished, Raspberry, R3

Bead Counts by Rounds
R1 - 18 seeds
R2 - 72 seeds
R3 - 180 seeds, 6 crystal
R4 - 108 seeds

Round 1
Pick up 18W, go with thread forward through the 1st W bead. Continue with thread around through all 18 W beads again coming out with thread at the 1st W bead.
Circle of 18 made, C18.

Round 2
a) Pick up 11W, go with thread forward through the 1 W bead in C18 that your working thread is exiting. Continue with thread forward through 3 more W beads in C18.
b) Pick up 11W, go with thread forward through the 1 W bead in C18 that your working thread is exiting, the 1st through 9th W beads just added in this step, and up through the 3rd W bead added in this Round at (a) or the previous repeat of (b) in this Round.
c) Pick up 1W, go with thread down through the 9th, 10th and 11th W beads, added in this Round at (b) and forward through 4 W beads in C18 as shown.
d) Continue R2 by repeating (b & c) around 3 more times. Repeat (b), 1 time.

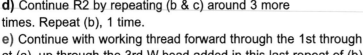

e) Continue with working thread forward through the 1st through 9th W beads added in this Round at (a), up through the 3rd W bead added in this last repeat of (b). Pick up 1W, go with thread down through the 9th, 10th, 11th W beads added in this Round at (a), 1 W bead in C18, up through the 1st, 2nd and 3rd W beads added in this Round at (a), and right to left through the 1 W bead added in this Round at the first repeat of (c).

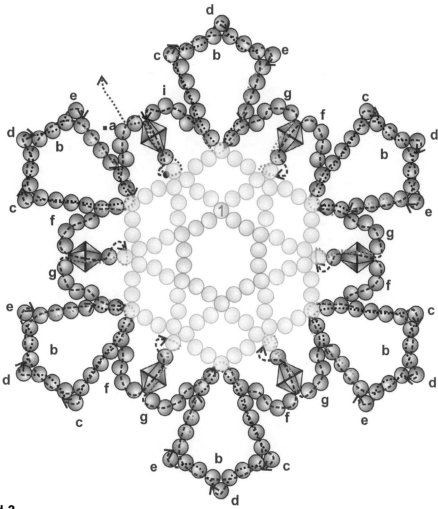

Round 3

a) Pick up 1W, 1C, 6W, go with thread right to left through the 6th W bead, R2(b).

b) Pick up 16W, go with thread down through the 5th and 6th W beads added in this Round at (a or g), right to left through the 6th W bead, R2(b), and forward through the 1st through 6th W beads just added in this step.

c) Pick up 1W, go with thread forward through the 7th, 8th and 9th W beads added in this Round at (b).

d) Pick up 1W, go with thread forward through the 10th, 11th and 12th W beads added in this Round at (b).

e) Pick up 1W, go with thread forward through the 13th through 16th W beads added in this Round at (b), the 5th, 6th W beads added in this Round at (a or g), right to left through the 6th W bead, R2(b), and up through the 1st and 2nd W beads added in this Round at (b).

f) Pick up 4W, 1C, 1W, go with thread right to left through the 1 W bead, R2(c), and up through the 1 W and 1 C beads just added in this step.

g) Pick up 6W, go with thread right to left through the 6th W bead, R2(b).

h) Continue R3 by repeating (b, c, d, e, f, g) around 4 more times. Repeat (b, c, d, e) 1 time.

i) Pick up 4W, go with thread down through the 1 C and 1 W beads added in this Round at (a), right to left through the 1 W bead, R2(c), up through the 1 W, 1 C and the 1st W (of the 6W) beads added in this Round at (a).

Round 4

a) Pick up 2W, go with thread up through the 1 W bead, R3(e).

b) Pick up 4W, go with thread right to left through the 1 W bead, R3(d).

c) Pick up 6W, go with thread forward through the 4th W bead added in this Round at (b), the 1 W bead, R3(d), and the 1st W bead just added in this step.

d) Pick up 3W, go with thread down through the 1W bead, R3(c).

e) Pick up 2W, go with thread right to left through the 4th W bead, R3(f or i).

f) Pick up 1W, go with thread right to left through the 1st W (of the 6W) bead, R3(g or a).

g) Continue R4 by repeating (a, b, c, d, e, f) around 5 more times.

h) Weave the working thread into the snowflake and finish off thread. Remove the stopper bead in the center and weave in and finish off thread.

SNOWFLAKE ORNAMENT #2
1-7/8 INCHES

W = Miyuki® 11/0 seed bead, #528, all Rounds

W = Miyuki® 11/0 seed bead, #10F R1, 3
Miyuki® 11/0 seed bead, #350, R2, 4
Please note: Ornament has only 4 Rounds

Bead Counts by Rounds
R1 - 48 seeds
R2 - 72 seeds
R3 - 60 seeds
R4 - 72 seeds
R5 - 48 seeds

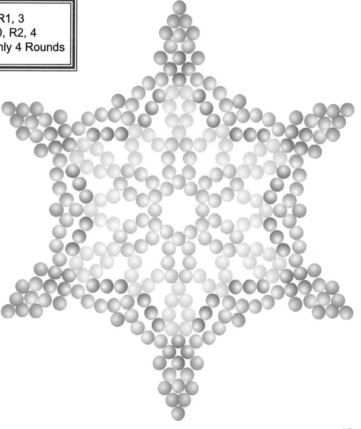

R1, a

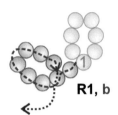

R1, b

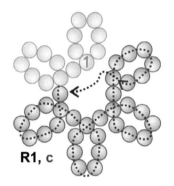

R1, c

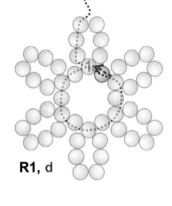

R1, d

Round 1

a) Pick up 7W, go with thread forward through the 1st W bead just added in this step.

b) Pick up 8W, go with thread forward through the 2nd W bead just added in this step.

c) Repeat (b) around 4 more times.

d) Pick up 1W, go with thread forward through the 1st W bead added in this Round at (a). Continue with working thread around through all the center beads as shown by the blue dotted line in diagram, then go with thread forward through the 1st W through 4th W beads added in this Round at (a).

This Round is worked clockwise

Round 2

a) Pick up 7W, go with thread down through the 1st W bead just added in this step and the 5th W bead added in R1(a) or the 6th W bead added in a repeat of R1(b).

b) Pick up 5W, go with thread up through the 5th W bead, R1(b) or the 4th W bead, R1(a).

c) Continue R2 by repeating (a, b) around 5 more times.

d) With working thread continue forward through the 1st through 4th W beads added in the first repeat of (a) this R.

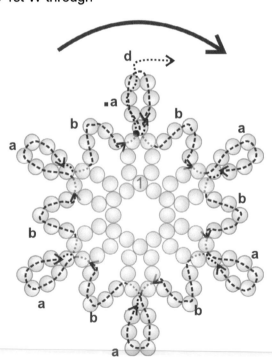

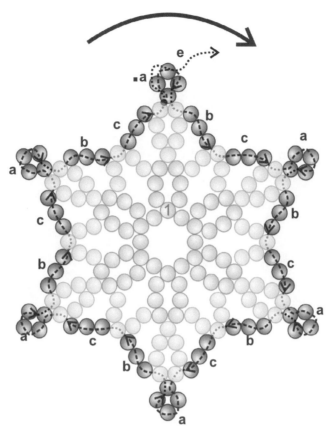

Round 3

a) Pick up 4W, go with thread down through the 1st W bead just added in this step and the 5th W bead, R2(a).

b) Pick up 3W, go with thread left to right through the 3rd W bead, R2(b).

c) Pick up 3W, go with thread up through the 4th W bead, R2(a).

d) Continue R3 by repeating (a, b, c) around 5 more times.

e) With working thread continue forward through the 1st, 2nd and 3rd W beads added in this R at the first repeat of (a).

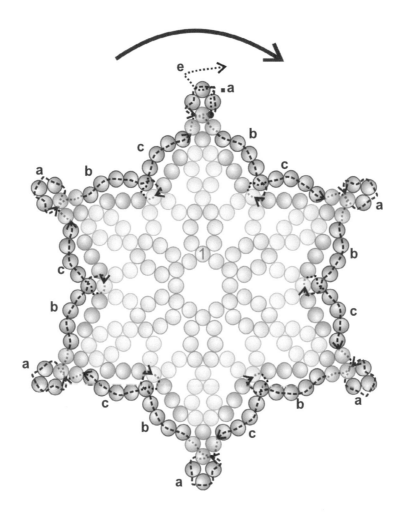

This Round is worked clockwise

Round 4

a) Pick up 3W, go with thread left to right through the 3rd and 4th W beads, R3(a).

b) Pick up 5W, go with thread right to left through the 3rd W bead, R2(b), and forward through the 5th W bead just added in this step.

c) Pick up 4W, go with thread forward through the 2nd and 3rd W beads, R3(a).

d) Continue R4 by repeating (a, b & c) around 5 more times.

e) With working thread continue forward through the 1st and 2nd W beads added in the first repeat of (a) this R.

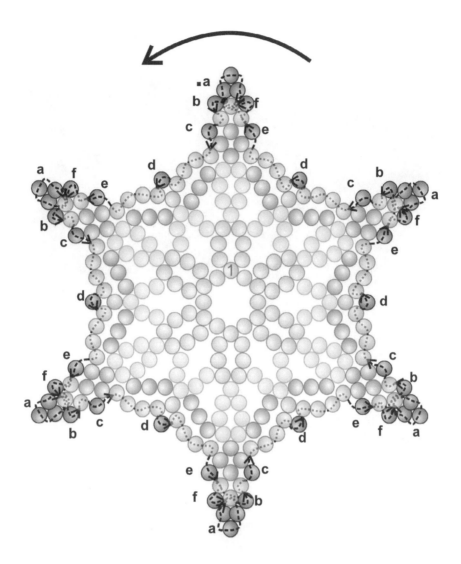

Round 5

a) Pick up 3W, go with thread right to left through the 2nd W bead, R4(a).

b) Pick up 1W, go with thread down through the 3rd W bead, R4(a).

c) Pick up 1W, go with thread right to left through the 4 W beads, R4(c).

d) Pick up 1W, go with thread through the 4th through 1st W beads, R4(b).

e) Pick up 1W, go with thread up through the 1st W bead, R4(a).

f) Pick up 1W, go with thread right to left through the 2nd W bead, R4(a).

g) Continue R5 by repeating (a, b, c, d, e, f) around 5 more times.

Weave the working thread into the snowflake and end.

SNOWFLAKE ORNAMENT #3
1-5/8 INCHES

W = Miyuki® 11/0 seed bead, #528, R1, 2, 3, 4
AB = Miyuki® 11/0 seed bead, #250, R5

W and AB = Miyuki® 11/0 seed bead, #1001,
all Rounds

Bead Counts by Rounds
R1 - 18 seeds
R2 - 30 seeds
R3 - 42 seeds
R4 - 72 seeds
R5 - 90 seeds

Round 1
Pick up 18W, go with thread forward through the 1st W bead. Continue with thread around through all 18 W beads again coming out with thread at the 1st W bead. Circle of 18 made, C18.

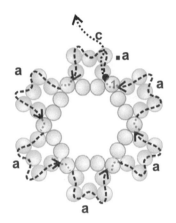

Round 2
a) Pick up 5AB, skip over 2 W beads and go with thread forward through the next 1 W bead in C18 as shown.
b) Continue R2 by repeating (a) around 5 more times.
c) With working thread continue forward through the 1st & 2nd AB beads, this Round at the first repeat of (a).

Round 3
a) Pick up 4W, go with thread down through the 2nd W bead just added in this step.
b) Pick up 1W, go with thread down through the 4th AB bead, R2(a).
c) Pick up 2W, go with thread up through the 2nd AB bead, next repeat to left of R2(a).
d) Continue R3 by repeating (a, b, c) around 5 more times.
e) With working thread continue forward (up) through the 1st, 2nd and 3rd W beads, this Round at the first repeat of (a).

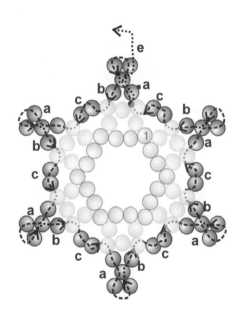

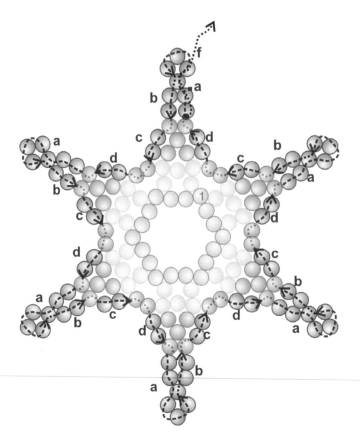

Round 4

a) Pick up 6W, go with thread down through the 3rd W bead just added in this step.

b) Pick up 2W, go with thread down through the 4th W bead, R3(a).

c) Pick up 2W, go with thread right to left through the 2 W beads, R3(c).

d) Pick up 2W, go with thread up through the 3rd W bead, R3(a).

e) Continue R4 by repeating (a, b, c, d) around 5 more times.

f) With working thread continue forward through the 1st, 2nd, 3rd and 4th W beads, this Round at the first repeat of (a).

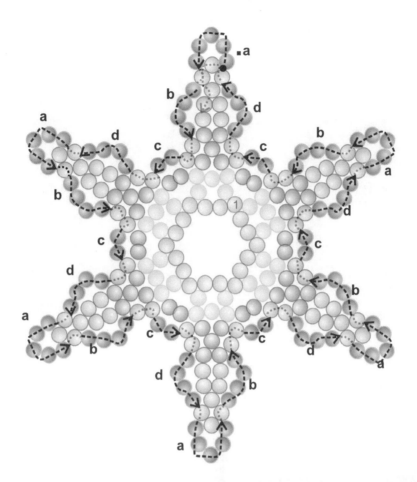

Round 5

a) Pick up 5AB, go with thread down through the 6th W bead, R4(a).

b) Pick up 4AB, go with thread down through the 2 W beads, R4(c).

c) Pick up 2AB, go with thread up through the 2 W beads, R4(d).

d) Pick up 4AB, go with thread up through the 4th W bead, R4(a).

e) Continue R5 by repeating (a, b, c, d) around 5 more times.

Weave the working thread into the snowflake and end.

SNOWFLAKE ORNAMENT #4
2 INCHES

W = Miyuki® 11/0 seed bead, #528, all Rounds
C = 4mm crystal AB. R3, 5
T = Miyuki® 10/0 triangle bead, crystal AB, R1

W = Miyuki® 11/0 seed bead, #1001, R1, 4, 5
     and Miyuki® 11/0 seed bead, #1340, R2
C = 4mm fire-polished, crystal AB. R3, 5
T = Miyuki® 10/0 triangle bead, #1140, R1

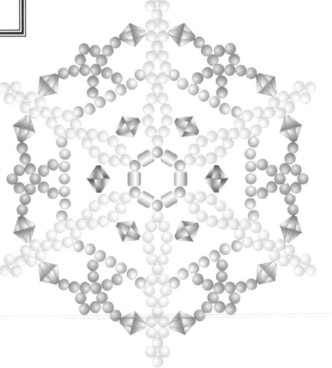

Bead Counts by Rounds
R1 - 6 seeds, 10/0 Triangle, 6
R2 - 150 seeds
R3 - 6 crystals
R4 - 42 seeds
R5 - 84 seeds, 12 crystals

Round 1

Pick up 1T, 1W, 1T, 1W, 1T, 1W, 1T, 1W, 1T, 1W, 1T, 1W, go with thread around through all 12 beads again, then go with thread forward through the 1st T and 1st W beads as shown.

Round 2

a) Pick up 16W, go with thread left to right (forward) through the 13th W bead just added in this step.
b) Pick up 2W, go with thread down through the 10th W bead added in this Round at (a).
c) Pick up 3W, go with thread down through the 6th W bead added in this Round at (a).
d) Pick up 4W, go with thread down through the 1st W bead added in this Round at (a) and forward through 1 W, 1 T, 1 W in R1 as shown..
e) Continue R2 by repeating (a, b, c, d) around 5 more times.
f) With working thread continue up through the 1st, 2nd and 3rd W beads added in the last repeat of (a) in this Round.

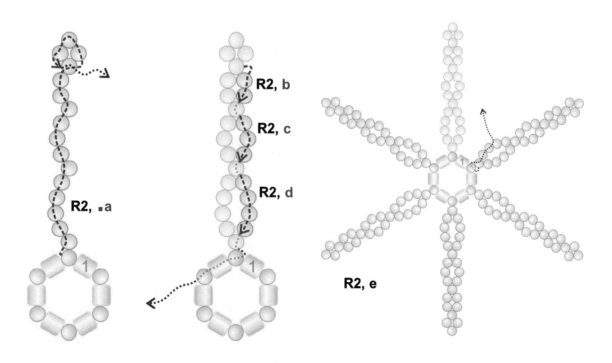

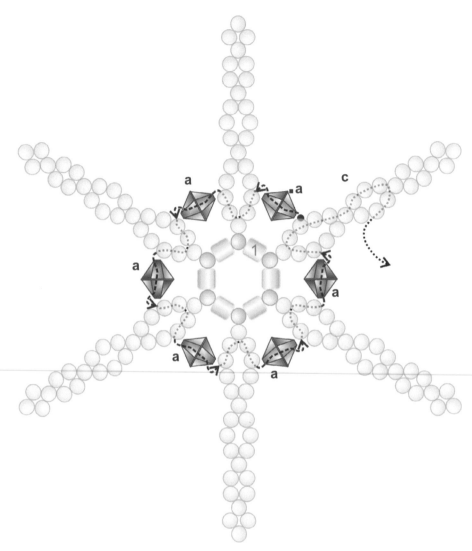

Round 3

a) Pick up 1C, go with thread down through the 3rd and 4th W beads, R2(d) and up through the 2nd and 3rd W beads, R2(a).

b) Continue R3 by repeating (a) around 5 more times.

c) With working thread continue by following the purple dotted line in diagram up then down coming out with thread down through the 1st and 2nd W beads, R2(c).

> **W** = Miyuki® 11/0 seed bead, #1920, all Rounds
> **C** = 4mm fire-polished, crystal AB. R3, 5
> **T** = Miyuki® 10/0 triangle bead, crystal AB, R1

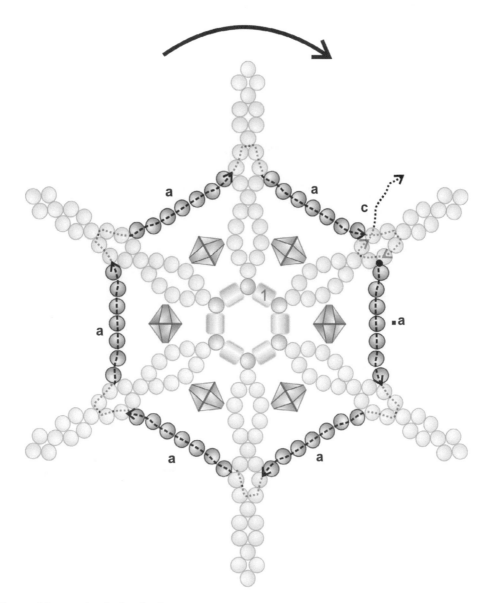

This Round is worked clockwise

Round 4

a) Pick up 7W, go with thread up through the 8th and 9th W beads, R2(a) and down through the 1st and 2nd W beads, R2(c).

b) Continue R4 by repeating (a) around 5 more times.

c) With working thread continue by following the purple dotted line in diagram, up then down, then up, coming out with thread up through the 8th W bead, R2(a), as shown.

Round 5

a) Pick up 1C, 6W, go with thread left to right through the 3rd, 4th and 5th W beads, R4(a).

b) Pick up 2W, go with thread forward (right to left) through the 4th W bead added in this Round at (a).

c) Pick up 4W, go with thread forward through the 3rd and 4th W beads added in this Round at (a), and the 1st W bead just added in this step.

d) Pick up 2W, 1C, go with thread down through the 2nd and 3rd W beads, R2(c), and up through the 7th and 8th W beads, R2(a).

e) Continue R5 by repeating (a, b, c, d) around 5 more times.

f) Weave the working thread into the snowflake and end.

Snowflake Ornament #5
2-1/2 Inches

W = Miyuki® 11/0 seed bead, #1920, R1, 3, 4, 6, 7
    Miyuki® 11/0 seed bead, #250, R2, 5
C = 4mm crystal AB. R4, 5

Bead Counts by Rounds

R1 - 12 seeds
R2 - 18 crystals
R3 - 54 seeds
R4 - 84 seeds, 6 crystals
R5 - 66 seeds, 6 crystals
R6 - 168 crystals
R7 - 84 seeds

Round 1
Pick up 12W, go with thread forward through the 1st W bead. Continue with thread around through all 12 W beads again coming out with thread at the 1st W bead. Circle of 12 made, C12.

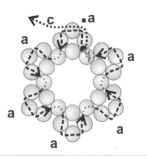

Round 2
a) Pick up 3W, skip over 1 W bead and go with thread through the next 1 W bead forward in C12.
b) Continue R2 by repeating (a) around 5 more times.
c) With working thread continue forward through the 1st & 2nd W beads, this Round at the first repeat of (a).

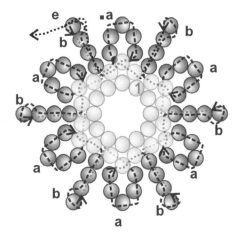

Round 3
a) Pick up 5W, go with thread forward through the 2nd and 3rd W beads, R2(a).
b) Pick up 4W, go with thread down through the 3rd, 2nd and 1st W beads just added in this step and forward through the 1st and 2nd W beads, next repeat, R2(a), left.
c) Continue R3 by repeating (a, b) around 5 more times.
d) With working thread continue forward through the 3rd W bead, R2(a), and up through the 4 W beads, this Round at the first repeat of (a).

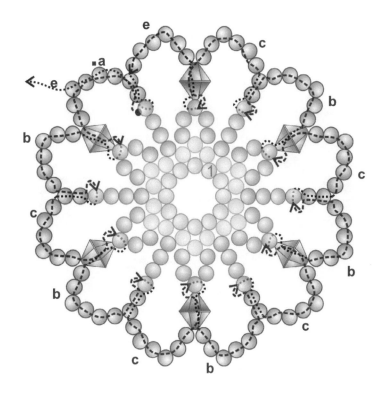

Round 4

a) Pick up 8W, 1C, go with thread right to left through the 3rd W bead, R3(a), and up through the 1 C bead just added in this step.

b) Pick up 8W, go with thread right to left through the 4th W bead, R3(b), and up through the 8th and 7th W beads just added in this step.

c) Pick up 6W, 1C, go with thread right to left through the 3rd W bead, next repeat, R3(a), left, and up through the C bead just added in this step.

d) Continue R4 by repeating (b, c) around 4 more times.

e) Pick up 6W, go with thread down through the 2nd and 1st W beads, added in this Round at (a), right to left through the 4th W bead, R3(b), and up (forward) through the 1st through 6th W beads added in the first repeat of (a) this R.

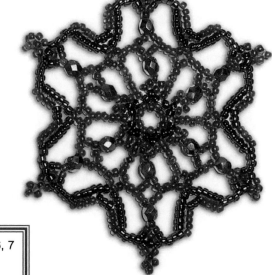

W = Miyuki® 11/0 seed bead, #1938, R1, 3, 4, 6, 7
       Miyuki® 11/0 seed bead, #1425, R2, 5
C = 4mm fire-polished, Silver. R4, 5

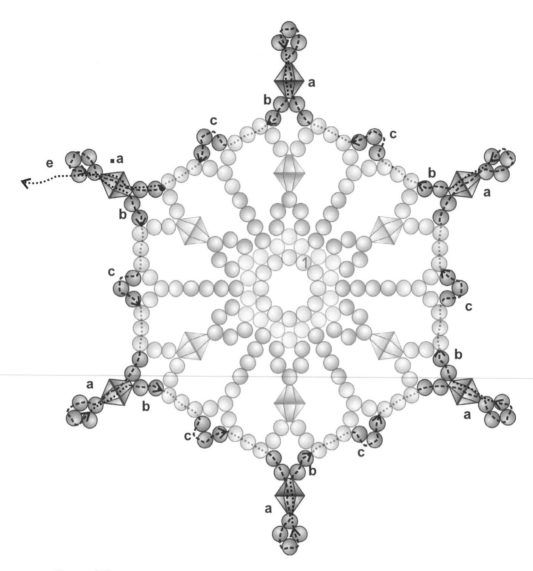

Round 5

a) Pick up 2W, 1C, 4W, go with thread down through the 1st W bead (of the 4W) and the 1 C beads just added in this step.

b) Pick up 2W, go with thread right to left through the 3rd, 4th and 5th W beads, R4(b or e).

c) Pick up 3W, go with thread right to left through the 2nd, 3rd and 4th W beads, R4(c) or the 4th, 5th and 6th W beads, R4(a).

d) Continue R5 by repeating (a, b, c) around 5 more times.

e) With working thread continue forward through the 2 W, 1 C, the 1st and 4th W beads (of the 4W) added in this Round at the first repeat of (a).

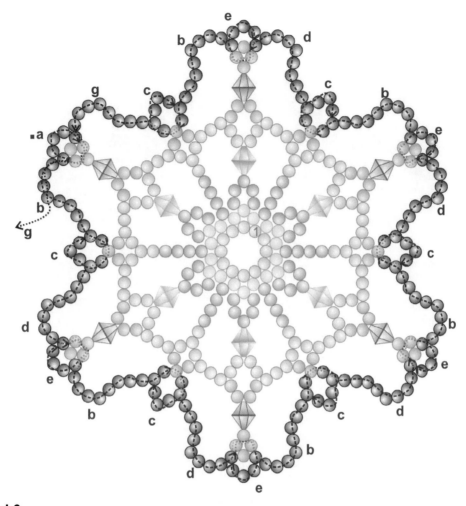

Round 6

a) Pick up 5W, go with thread down through the 2nd W bead and up through the 4th W bead, R5(a), and up through the 1st W bead just added in this step.

b) Pick up 10W, go with thread right to left through the 2nd W bead, R5(c).

c) Pick up 5W, go with thread down through the 9th and 10th W beads, added in this Round at (b), right to left through the 2nd W bead, R5(c), and up through the 1st and 2nd W beads just added in this step.

d) Pick up 9W, go with thread down through the 2nd W bead and up through the 4th W bead, next repeat R5(a), left.

e) Pick up 4W, go with thread down through the 9th W bead, this Round at (d), the 2nd W bead and up through the 4th W bead, R5(a), and up through the 1st W bead just added in this step.

f) Continue R6 by repeating (b, c, d, e) around 4 more times. Repeat (b & c) 1 time.

g) Pick up 8W, go with thread down through the 5th W bead added in this Round at (a), down through the 2nd W bead and up through the 4th W bead, R5(a), this 1st W bead added in this Round at (a), and forward through the 1st through 4th W beads added in the last repeat of (b), this Round.

Round 7

a) Pick up 4W, go with thread right to left through the 5th, 4th and 3rd W beads, R6(c).

b) Pick up 4W, go with thread right to let through the 5th, 6th, 7th and 8th W beads, R6(d), and up through the 4th W bead, R6(e or a).

c) Pick up 5W, go with thread forward through the 2nd W bead just added in this step.

d) Pick up 1W, go with thread down through the 2nd W bead, R6(e or a), and right to left through the 1st through 4th W beads, R6(b).

e) Continue R7 by repeating (a, b, c, d) around 5 more times.

g) Weave the working thread into the snowflake and end.

W = Miyuki® 11/0 seed bead, #528, R1, 2, 3, 5, 6
      Miyuki® 11/0 seed bead, #250, R4
C = 4mm crystal AB, R3

W = Miyuki® 11/0 seed bead, #1938, R1, 3, 4
      Miyuki® 11/0 seed bead, #1436, R2, 5, 6
C = No crystals are used in this sample, I substituted
      #1436, see Round 3 optional step (a), page 39

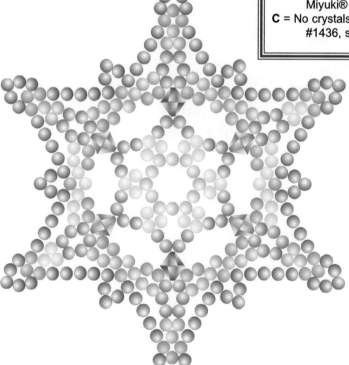

Bead Counts by Rounds
R1 - 12 seed
R2 - 18 seed
R3 - 60 seed, 6 crystals
R4 - 60 seed
R5 - 48 seed
R6 - 108 seed

Round 1
Pick up 12W, go with thread forward through the 1st W bead. Continue with thread around through all 12 W beads again coming out with thread at the 1st W bead. Circle of 12 made, C12.

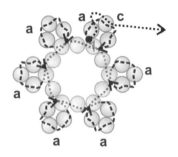

Round 2
a) Pick up 3W, go with thread forward through the 1 W bead your working thread is exiting and 2 more W beads in C12.
b) Continue R2 by repeating (a) around 5 more times.
c) With working thread continue forward through the 1st and 2nd W beads just added in this Round at the first repeat of (a).

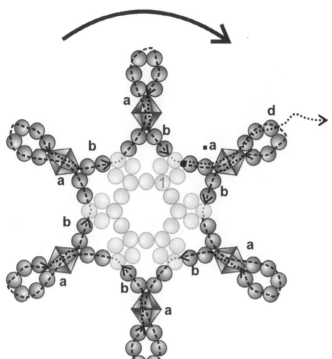

This Round is worked clockwise
Round 3
a) Pick up 2W, 1C, 6W, go with thread down through the 1 C bead just added in this step.
b) Pick up 2W, go with thread left to right through the 2nd W bead, R2(a).
c) Continue R3 by repeating (a & b) around 5 more times.
d) Continue with working thread forward through the 2 W, 1 C, 1st, 2nd and 3rd W beads in the first repeat of (a) this Round.

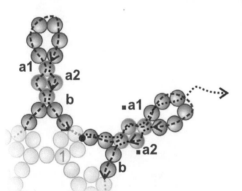

Optional Step (a) without crystals for the Pink and Green Snowflake
Round 3
a1) Pick up 2 green, 3 pink, 6 green, go with thread down through the 3rd pink bead just added in this step.
a2) Pick up 1 pink, go with thread down through the 1st pink bead, added in this Round at (a1).
b) Pick up 2 green, go with thread left to right through the 2nd W bead, R2(a).
c) Continue R3 by repeating (a1, a2 & b) around 5 more times.
d) Continue with working thread forward through the 1st and 2nd green, the 3 pink, and the 1st, 2nd and 3rd green beads in the first repeat of (a1) this Round.

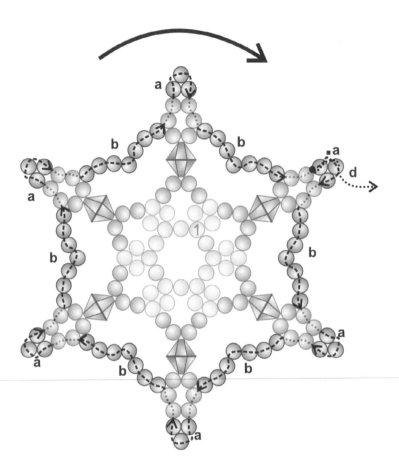

This Round is worked clockwise

Round 4

a) Pick up 3W, go with thread down through the 4th and 5th W beads, R3(a).

b) Pick up 7W, go with thread up through the 2nd and 3rd W beads added in the next repeat of (a), R3.

c) Continue R4 by repeating (a & b) around 5 more times.

d) With working thread continue forward through the 1st & 2nd W beads added in the first repeat of (a) this Round.

W = Miyuki® 11/0 seed bead, #1920,
  R1, 2, 3, 5, 6
  Miyuki® 11/0 seed bead, #250, R3
C = 4mm fire-polished, crystal AB, R3

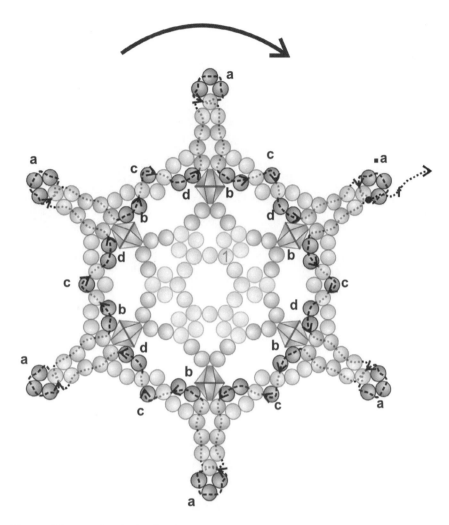

This Round is worked clockwise

Round 5

a) Pick up 3W, go with thread left to right through the 2nd W bead and down through the 3rd W bead, R4(a), continue down through the 4th, 5th and 6th W beads, R3(a).

b) Pick up 2W, go with thread left to right through the 3rd W bead, R4(b).

c) Pick up 1W, go with thread left to right through the 5th W bead, R4(b).

d) Pick up 2W, go with thread up through the 1st, 2nd and 3rd W beads, R3(a), the 1st W and left to right through the 2nd W bead, R4(a).

e) Continue R5 by repeating (a, b, c & d) around 5 more times.

f) With working thread continue up through the 1st W bead added in the first repeat of (a) this Round.

This Round is worked counter-clockwise

Round 6

a) Pick up 5W, go with thread down through the 3rd W bead, R5(a).

b) Pick up 5W, go with thread left to right through the 1 W bead, R5(c).

c) Pick up 4W, go with thread left to right through the 5th W bead added in this Round at (b), the 1 W bead, R5(c), and the 1st W bead just added in this step.

d) Pick up 4W, go with thread up through the 1st W bead, R5(a) in the next repeat to the left.

e) Continue R6 by repeating (a, b, c & d) around 5 more times.

f) Weave the working threads into the snowflake and end.

SNOWFLAKE ORNAMENT #7
1 7/8 INCHES

```
W  = Miyuki® 11/0 seed bead, #528, R1, 2, 3, 4
AB = Miyuki® 11/0 seed bead, #250, R5, 6
C  = 4mm crystal AB, R2
```

```
W = Miyuki® 11/0 seed bead, #25F, all Rounds
C = 4mm fire-polished, gold
```

Bead Counts by Rounds
R1 - 18 seed
R2 - 6 seed, 6 crystals
R3 - 84 seed
R4 - 78 seed
R5 - 66 seed
R6 - 72 seed

Round 1

Pick up 18W, go with thread forward through the 1st W bead. Continue with thread around through all 18 W beads again coming out with thread at the 3rd W bead. Circle of 18 made, C18.

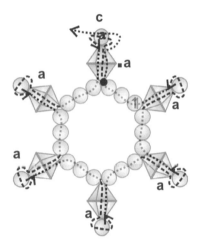

Round 2,

a) Pick up 1C, 1W, go with thread down through the 1 C bead just added in this step, and forward through 3 W beads in C18 as shown.
b) Continue R2 by repeating (a) around 5 more times.
c) With working thread continue forward through the 1 C and 1 W beads just added in this Round at the first repeat of (a).

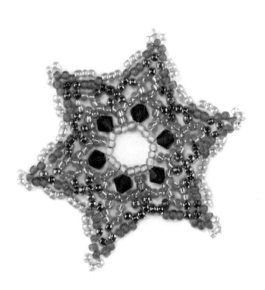

W = Miyuki® 11/0 seed bead, #1920, all Rounds
C = 4mm fire-polished, crystal AB, R2

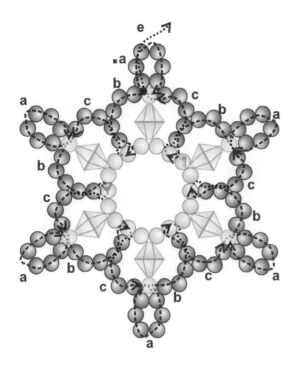

Round 3

a) Pick up 6W, go with thread right to left through the 1 W bead, R2(a).

b) Pick up 5W, go with thread right to left through the 1 W bead in C18 as shown and up through the 5th and 4th W beads just added in this step.

c) Pick up 3W, go with thread right to left through the 1 W bead added in the next repeat left, R2(a).

d) Continue R3 by repeating (a, b, c) around 5 more times.

e) With working thread continue forward through the 1st, 2nd and 3rd W beads just added in this Round at the first repeat of (a).

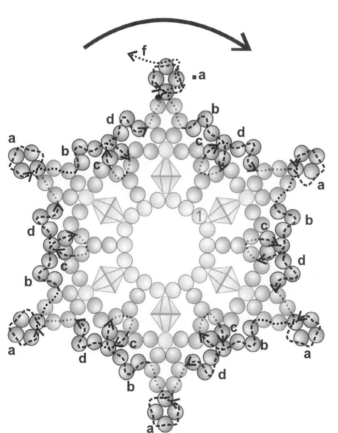

This Round is worked clockwise

Round 4

a) Pick up 4W, go with thread forward through the 1st W bead just added in this step, and down through the 4th and 5th W beads, R3(a).

b) Pick up 5W, go with thread down through the 3rd W bead, R3(b), and up through the 1st W bead, R3(c).

c) Pick up 1W, go with thread left to right through the 4th W bead added in this Round at (b).

d) Pick up 3W, go with thread up through the 2nd and 3rd W beads, R3(a).

e) Continue R4 by repeating (a, b, c, d) around 5 more times.

f) With working thread continue forward through the 1st, 2nd and 3rd W beads just added in this Round at the first repeat of (a).

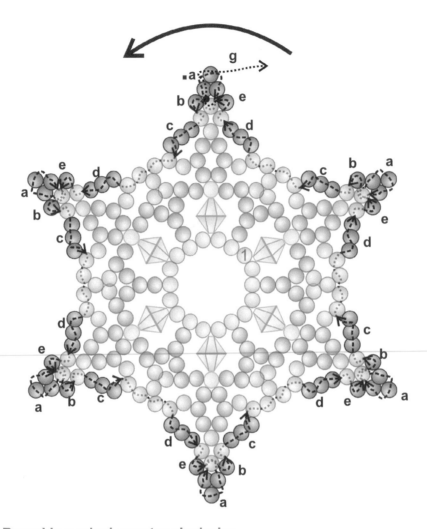

This Round is worked counter-clockwise

Round 5

a) Pick up 3W, go with thread right to left through the 3rd W bead, R4(a).

b) Pick up 1W, go with thread down through the 4th W bead, R4(a).

c) Pick up 3W, go with thread right to left through the 2nd and 1st W beads, R4(d), and the 3rd and 2nd W beads, R4(b).

d) Pick up 3W, go with thread up through the 2nd W bead, R4(a).

e) Pick up 1W, go with thread right to left through the 3rd W bead, R4(a).

f) Continue R5 by repeating (a, b, c, d, e) around 5 more times.

g) With working thread continue forward through the 1st and 2nd W beads, this Round at the first repeat of (a).

Round 6

a) Pick up 3W, go with thread left to right, then down through the 2nd and 3rd W beads, R5(a), and the 1 W bead, R5(e).

b) Pick up 3W, go with thread left to right through the 1st W bead, R5(d).

c) Pick up 3W, go with thread left to right through the 3rd W bead, R5(c).

d) Pick up 3W, go with thread up through the 1 W bead, R5(b), up, then left to right through the 1st and 2nd W beads, R5(a).

e) Continue R6 by repeating (a, b, c, d) around 5 more times. Weave the working thread into the snowflake and end.

Snowflake Ornament #8
1-3/4 Inches

W = Miyuki® 11/0 seed bead, #1920, all Rounds
C = 4mm crystal AB, R3

W = Miyuki® 11/0 seed bead, #577, all Rounds
C = 4mm fire-polished, gold, R3

Bead Counts by Rounds
R1 - 78 seeds
R2 - 60 seeds
R3 - 60 seeds, 6 crystal
R4 - 72 seeds

R1, a

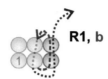 **R1, b**

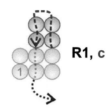 **R1, c**

R1, d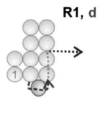

R1, e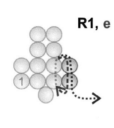

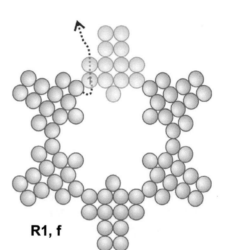

R1, f

Round 1

a) Pick up 4W, go with thread forward through the 4 W beads just added in this step. Stack the beads as shown in the diagram.

b) Pick up 2W, go with thread down through the 3rd and 4th W beads added at (a), and up through the 2 W beads just added in this step.

c) Pick up 4W, go with thread down through the 3rd and 4th W beads added at (a).

d) Pick up 1W, go with thread up through the 2 W beads added at (b).

e) Pick up 2W, go with thread up through the 2 W beads added at (b) and down through the 2 W beads just added in this step.

f) Continue R1 by repeating (a, b, c, d, e) around 5 more times.

g) With working thread continue up through the 1st and 2nd W beads added in the first repeat of (a) in this Round.

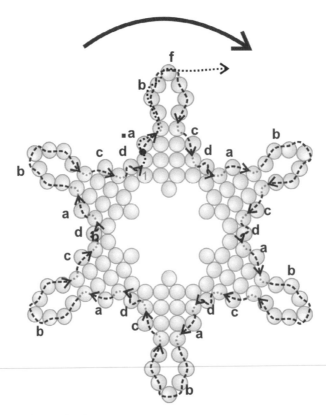

Round 2

a) Pick up 1W, go with thread up through the 3rd W bead, R1(c).

b) Pick up 7W, go with thread down through the 2nd W bead, R1(c).

c) Pick up 1W, go with thread down through the 1st W bead, R1(e).

d) Pick up 1W, go with thread up through the 2nd W bead in the next right repeat, R1(a).

e) Continue R2 by repeating (a, b, c, d) around 5 more times.

f) With working thread continue forward through the 1st W bead added in this Round at the first repeat of (a), up through the 3rd W bead, R1(c), and the 1st through 4th W beads, this Round at the first repeat of (b).

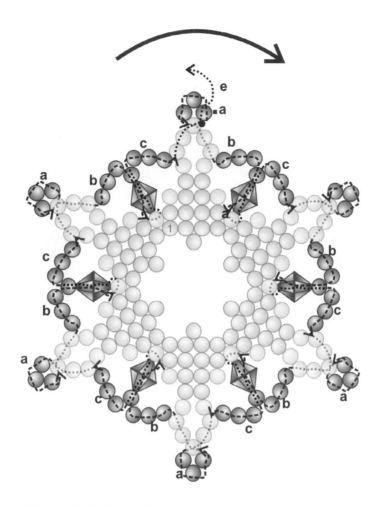

Round 3

a) Pick up 3W, go with thread left to right, then down through the 4th, 5th and 6th W bead, R2(b).

b) Pick up 4W, 1C, go with thread left to right through the 1 W bead, R2(d), and up through the 1 C and 4th W beads just added in this step.

c) Pick up 3W, go with thread up, then left to right through the 2nd, 3rd and 4th W beads in the next repeat right, R2(b).

d) Continue R3 by repeating (a, b, c) around 5 more times.

e) With working thread continue up through the 1st W bead added in this Round at the first repeat of (a).

This Round is worked counter-clockwise

Round 4

a) Pick up 5W, go with thread down through the 3rd W beads, R3(a).

b) Pick up 2W, go with thread right to left through the 2nd and 1st W beads, R3(c).

c) Pick up 3W, go with thread right to left through the 3rd and 2nd W beads, R3(b).

d) Pick up 2W, go with thread up through the 1st W bead in the next repeat left, R3(a).

e) Continue R4 by repeating (a, b, c, d) around 5 more times.

Weave the working thread into the snowflake and end.

SNOWFLAKE ORNAMENT #9
2 1/8 INCHES

W = Miyuki® 11/0 seed bead, #284, R2, 3, 5, 7
AB = Miyuki® 11/0 seed bead, #250, R1, 4, 6, 8

W = Miyuki® 11/0 seed bead, #4, R2, 3, 5, 7
AB = Miyuki® 11/0 seed bead, #350, R1, 4, 6, 8

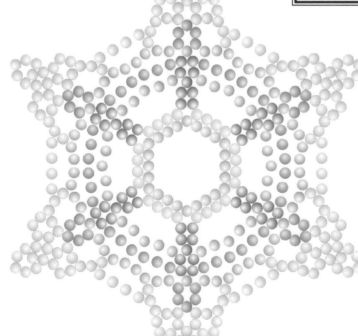

Bead Counts by Rounds
R1 - 24 seed
R2 - 24 seed
R3 - 54 seed
R4 - 36 seed
R5 - 66 seed
R6 - 46 seed
R7 - 96 seed
R8 - 90 seed

Round 1

Pick up 24AB, go with thread forward through the 1st AB bead. Continue with thread around through all 24 AB beads again coming out with thread at the 1st AB bead. Circle of 24 made, C24.

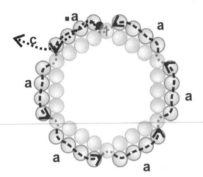

Round 2,

a) Pick up 4W, skip over 3 AB and go with thread forward through the next AB bead in C24 as shown.
b) Continue R2 by repeating (a) around 5 more times.
c) With working thread continue forward through the 4 W beads added in this Round at the first repeat of (a).

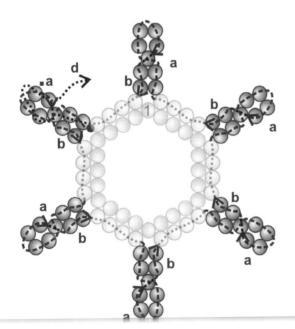

Round 3

a) Pick up 7W, go with thread forward through the 3rd W bead just added in this step.
b) Pick up 2W, go with thread forward (right to left) through the next set of 4 W beads, R2(a).
c) Continue R3 by repeating (a, b) around 5 more times.
d) With working thread continue up and around through the 7 W beads added in this Round at the first repeat of (a).

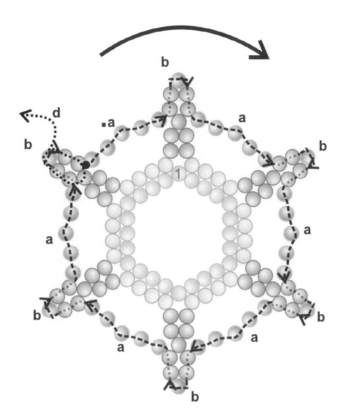

This Round is worked clockwise

Round 4

a) Pick up 5AB, go with thread up through the 4th and 5th W beads, R3(a).

b) Pick up 1AB, go with thread down through the 6th and 7th W beads, R3(a).

d) Continue R4 by repeating (a, b) around 5 more times.

e) With working thread continue around through the 3rd, 4th and 5th W beads, R3(a), and left to right through the 1 AB bead added in this Round at the last repeat of (b).

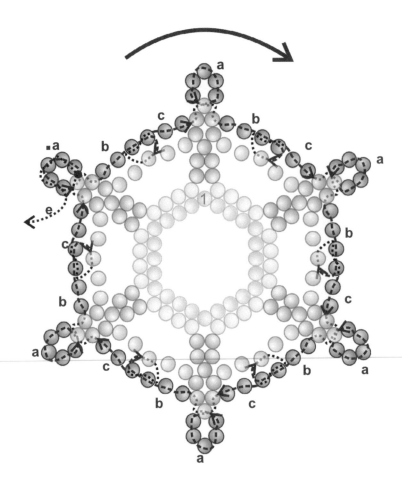

This Round is worked clockwise

Round 5

a) Pick up 5W, go with thread left to right through the 1 AB bead, R4(b), and down through the 6th W bead, R3(a).

b) Pick up 4W, go with thread right to left through the 3rd AB bead, R4(a), and left to right through the 3rd and 4th W beads just added in this step.

c) Pick up 2W, go with thread up through the 5th W bead, R3(a), and left to right through the 1 AB bead, R4(b).

d) Continue R5 by repeating (a, b, c) around 5 more times.

e) With working thread continue forward through the 5 W beads added in this Round at the first repeat of (a).

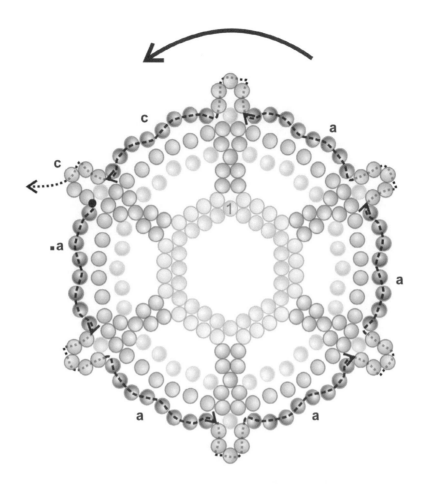

Round 6

a) Pick up 8AB, go with thread up, then down through the 5 W beads, in the next repeat to left, R5(a).

b) Continue R6 by repeating (a) around 4 more times.

c) Pick up 8AB, go with thread up through the 1st, 2nd and 3rd W beads, in the next repeat to left, R5(a).

W = Miyuki® 11/0 seed bead, #1920, R2, 3, 5, 7
AB = Miyuki® 11/0 seed bead, #250, R1, 4, 6, 8

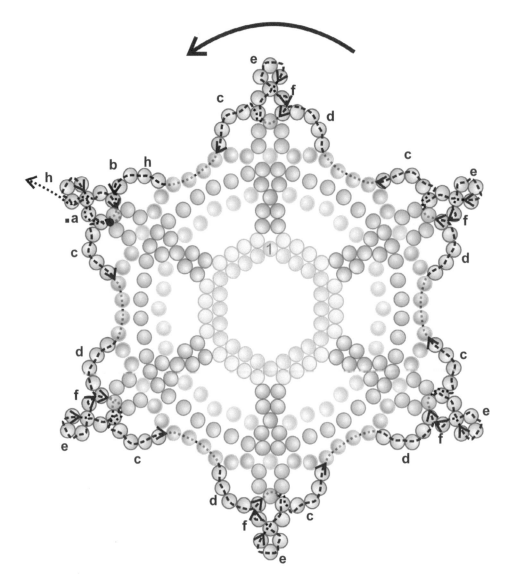

Round 7

a) Pick up 6W, go with thread down through the 3rd W bead just added in this step.

b) Pick up 2W, go with thread right to left through with 3rd W bead, R5(a), and up through the 1st W bead added in this Round at (a).

c) Pick up 4W, go with thread right to left through the 3rd, 4th, 5th and 6th AB beads, R6(a).

d) Pick up 5W, go with thread right to left through the 3rd W bead, R5(a).

e) Pick up 6W, go with thread down through the 3rd W bead just added in this step.

f) Pick up 1W, go with thread right to left through the 5th W bead, added in this Round at (d), right to left through the 3rd W bead, R5(a), and up through the 1st W bead added in this Round at (e).

g) Continue R7 by repeating (c, d, e, f) around 4 more times. Repeat (c), 1 time.

h) Pick up 4W, go with thread down through the 2nd W bead added in this Round at (b), right to left through the 3rd W bead, R5(a), and up through the 1st through 4th W beads added in this Round at the first repeat of (a).

This Round is worked clockwise

Round 8

a) Pick up 5AB, go with thread down through the 6th W bead, R7(a or e).

b) Pick up 3AB, go with thread down through the 3rd and 2nd W beads, R7(d or h).

c) Pick up 4AB, go with thread up through the 3rd and 2nd W beads, R7(c).

d) Pick up 3AB, go with thread up through the 4th W bead, R7(e or a).

e) Continue R8 by repeating (a, b, c, d) around 5 more times.

Weave the working thread into the snowflake and end.

SNOWFLAKE ORNAMENT #10
2 INCHES

W = Miyuki® 11/0 seed bead, #528, R2, R3, R4
AB = Miyuki® 11/0 seed bead, #250, R1, R5, R6
C = 4mm crystal AB, R2

Miyuki® 11/0 seed bead, #250, all Rounds
4mm fire-polished, crystal AB
*This sample snowflake stops after
  completeing Round 5

Bead Counts by Rounds
R1 - 24 seed
R2 - 48 seed, 12 crystal
R3 - 90 seed
R4 - 90 seed
R5 - 78 seed
R6 - 84 seed

Round 1
Pick up 24AB, go with thread forward through the 1st AB bead. Continue with thread around through all 24 AB beads again coming out with thread at the 1st AB bead. Circle of 24 made, C24.

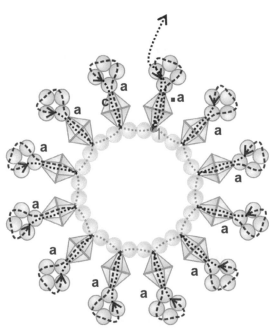

Round 2
a) Pick up 1C, 4W, go with thread down through the 1st W and 1 C beads just added in this step and forward through 2 AB beads in C24, R1 as shown.
b) Continue R2 by repeating (a) around 11 more times.
c) With working thread continue up through the 1 C and the 1st and 4th W beads just added in this Round at the first repeat of (a).

Miyuki® 11/0 seed bead, #1920, all Rounds
4mm fire-polished, crystal AB, R2

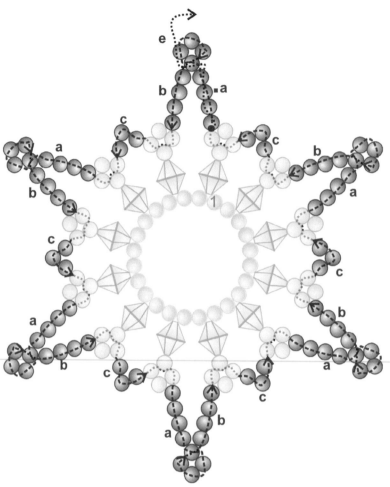

Round 3

a) Pick up 8W, go with thread forward through the 5th W bead just added in this step.

b) Pick up 4W, go with thread down through the 2nd W and up through the 4th W beads, in the next repeat to left, R2(a).

c) Pick up 3W, go with thread down through the 2nd W and up through the 4th W beads, in the next repeat to left, R2(a).

d) Continue R3 by repeating (a, b, c) around 5 more times.

e) With working thread continue forward through the 1st through 6th W beads added in this Round at the first repeat of (a).

This Round is worked clockwise

Round 4

a) Pick up 5W, go with thread down through the 8th W bead, R3(a).

b) Pick up 4W, go with thread left to right through the 3rd W bead, R2(a).

c) Pick up 1W, go with thread left to right through the 2nd W bead, R3(c).

d) Pick up 1W, go with thread left to right through the 3rd W bead, in the next repeat to right, R2(a).

e) Pick up 4W, go with thread up through the 6th W bead, R3(a).

f) Continue R4 by repeating (a, b, c, d, e) around 5 more times.

g) With working thread continue forward through the 1st, 2nd and 3rd W beads added in this Round at the first repeat of (a).

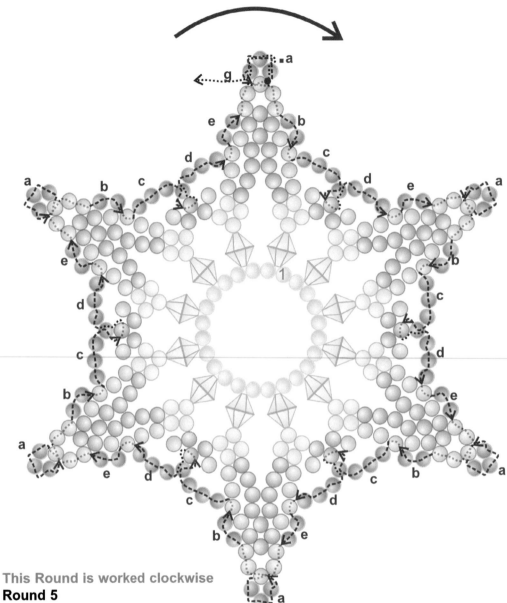

This Round is worked clockwise

Round 5

a) Pick up 3AB go with thread left
to right through the 3rd, then down through the 4th and 5th W beads, R4(a).

b) Pick up 2AB, go with thread down through the 2nd W bead, R4(b).

c) Pick up 4AB, go with thread right to left through the 2nd W bead, R3(c), and up
through the 4th AB bead just added in this step.

d) Pick up 3AB, go with thread go with thread up through the 3rd W bead, R4(e).

e) Pick up 2AB, go with thread up and left to right through the 1st,
2nd and 3rd W beads, R4(a).

e) Continue R5 by repeating (a, b, c, d, e) around 5 more times.

f) With working thread continue forward through the 3 AB beads,
this Round at the first repeat of (a).

This Round is worked counter-clockwise

Round 6

a) Pick up 4AB, go with thread down through the 1st AB bead, R5(e).

b) Pick up 1AB, go with thread right to left through the 3 AB beads, R5(d), and the 3rd AB bead, R5(c).

c) Pick up 3AB, go with thread right to left through the 1st AB bead, R5(d), and the 3rd, 2nd and 1st AB beads, R5(c).

d) Pick up 1AB, go with thread up through the 2nd AB bead, R5(b).

e) Pick up 4AB, go with thread through the 1st, 2nd and 3rd AB beads, R5(a).

f) Continue R6 by repeating (a, b, c, d, e) around 5 more times.

Weave the working thread into the snowflake and end.

SNOWFLAKE ORNAMENT #11
2 1/4 INCHES

W = Miyuki® 11/0 seed bead, #528, R1, 2, 4, 5
AB = Miyuki® 11/0 seed bead, #250, R3, 6
C = 4mm crystal AB, R3, 4

W = Miyuki® 11/0 seed bead, #1924, all Rounds
C = 4mm fire-polished, light blue, R3, 4

Bead Counts by Rounds
R1 - 18 seed
R2 - 60 seed
R3 - 78 seed, 6 crystal
R4 - 78 seed, 6 crystal
R5 - 84 seed
R6 - 108 seed

Round 1

Pick up 18W, go with thread forward through the 1st W bead. Continue with thread around through all 18 W beads again coming out with thread at the 1st W bead. Circle of 18 made, C18.

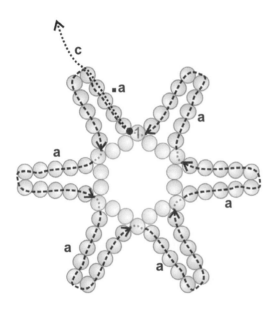

Round 2

a) Pick up 10W, skip over 2 W bead and go with thread forward through the next 1 W bead in C18, R1.

b) Continue R2 by repeating (a) around 5 more times.

c) With working thread continue forward through the 1st through 5th W beads, this Round at the first repeat of (a).

W = Miyuki® 11/0 seed bead, #1920, all Rounds
C = 4mm fire-polished, crystal AB, R3, R4

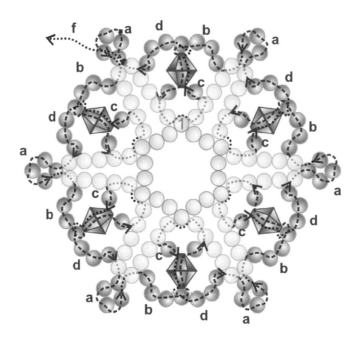

Round 3

a) Pick up 4AB, go with thread down through the 1st AB bead just added in this step and the 6th W bead, R2(a).

b) Pick up 4AB, 1C, 1AB, go with thread down through the 2nd and 1st W beads in the left repeat of R2(a), and up through the 10th and 9th W beads in the right repeat of R2(a).

c) Pick up 1AB, go with thread up through the 1 C bead and right to left through the 4th A bead just added in this Round at (b).

d) Pick up 3AB, go with thread up through the 5th W bead in the left repeat of R2(a).

e) Continue R3 by repeating (a, b, c, d) around 5 more times.

f) With working thread continue forward through the 1st and 4th AB beads, this Round at the first repeat of (a).

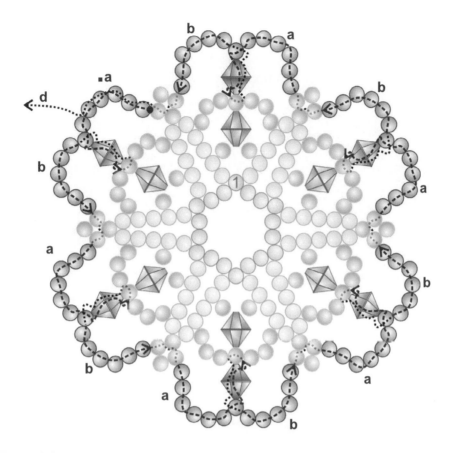

Round 4

a) Pick up 7W, 1C, go with thread through the 4th AB bead, R3(b), up through the 1 C bead just added in this step, and right to left (forward) through the 7th W bead just added in this step.

b) Pick up 6W, go with thread down through the 2nd AB bead and up through the 4th AB bead, R3(a).

c) Continue R4 by repeating (a, b) around 5 more times.

d) With working thread continue forward through the 1st through 5th W beads just added in this Round at the first repeat of (a).

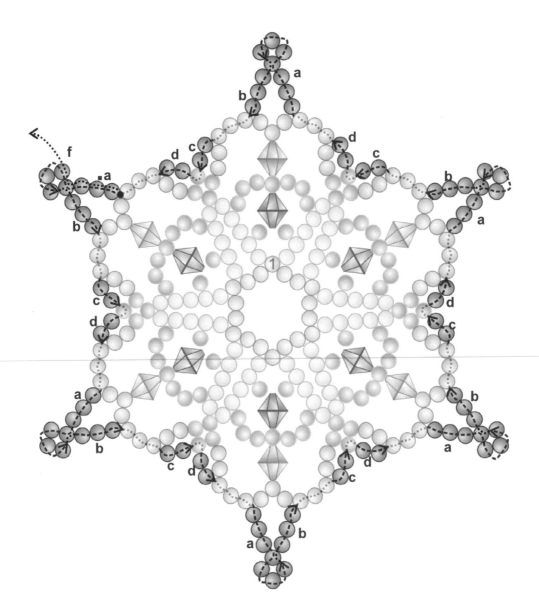

Round 5

a) Pick up 7W, go with thread down through the 4th W bead just added in this step.

b) Pick up 3W, go with thread right to left through the 2nd, 3rd and 4th W beads, R4(b).

c) Pick up 2W, go with thread right to left through he 3rd AB bead, R3(a).

d) Pick up 2W, go with thread right to left through the 3rd, 4th and 5th W beads, R4(a).

e) Continue R5 by repeating (a, b, c, d) around 5 more times.

f) With working thread continue forward through the 1st through 5th W beads added in this Round at the first repeat of (a).

Round 6

a) Pick up 5AB, go with thread down through the 7th W bead, R5(a).

b) Pick up 6AB, go with thread right to left through the 2 W beads, R5(c).

c) Pick up 1AB, go with thread right to left through the 2 W beads, R5(d).

d) Pick up 6AB, go with thread up through the 5th W bead, R5(a).

e) Continue R6 by repeating (a, b, c, d) around 5 more times.

Weave the working thread into the snowflake and end.

SNOWFLAKE ORNAMENT #12
2 3/4 INCHES

Bead Counts by Rounds
R1 - 12 seeds
R2 - 18 seeds
R3 - 66 seeds, 6 crystal
R4 - 66 seeds
R5 - 84 seeds
R6 - 84 seeds
R7 - 150 seeds, 6 crystal
R8 - 114 seeds
R9 - 120 seeds

W = Miyuki® 11/0 seed bead, #528,
R1, 2, 3, 6, 7, 8, 9
AB = Miyuki® 11/0 seed bead, #250, 4, 5
C = 4mm crystal AB, R3, 7

W = Miyuki® 11/0 seed bead, #353,
R1, 2, 3, 6, 7, 8, 9
AB = Miyuki® 11/0 seed bead, #1001, R4, 5
C = 4mm fire-polished, crystal AB, R3, 7

Round 1

Pick up 12W, go with thread forward through the 1st W bead. Continue with thread around through all 12 W beads again coming out with thread at the 1st W bead. Circle of 12 made, C12.

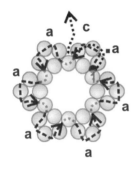

Round 2

a) Pick up 3W, skip over 1 W bead and go with thread through the next 1 W bead forward in C12 as shown.
b) Continue R2 by repeating (a) around 5 more times.
c) With working thread continue forward through the 3 W beads, added in this Round at the first repeat of (a).

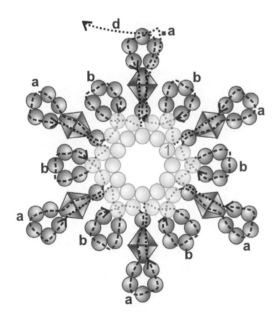

Round 3

a) Pick up 1W, 1C, 5W, go with thread down through the 1 C and 1 W beads just added in this step, and right to left through the 1st and 2nd W beads, R2(a).
b) Pick up 5W, go with thread right to left through the 2nd and 3rd W beads, R2(a).
c) Continue R3 by repeating (a, b) around 5 more times.
d) With working thread continue up through the 1 W, 1 C and the 1st, 2nd and 3rd W beads added in this Round at the first repeat of (a).

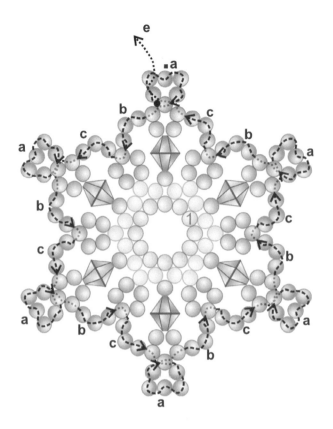

Round 4

a) Pick up 5AB, go with thread right to left through the 3rd and 4th W beads, R3(a).

b) Pick up 3AB, go with thread right to left through the 3rd W bead, R3(b).

c) Pick up 3AB, go with thread right to left through the 2nd and 3rd W beads, next repeat left, R3(a).

d) Continue R4 by repeating (a, b, c) around 5 more times.

e) With working thread continue forward through the 1st and 2nd AB beads just added in this Round at the first repeat of (a).

> **W** = Miyuki® 11/0 seed bead, #284,
>   R1, 2, 3, 5, 6, 7
> **AB** = Miyuki® 11/0 seed bead, #250, R4, 8, 9
> **C** = 4mm fire-polished, crystal AB, R3, 7

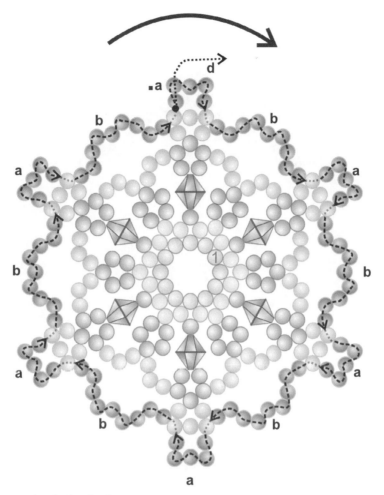

This Round is worked clockwise

Round 5

a) Pick up 5AB, go with thread down through the 4th AB bead, R4(a).

b) Pick up 9AB, go with thread up through the 2nd AB bead, next repeat right, R4(a).

c) Continue R5 by repeating (a, b) around 5 more times.

d) With working thread continue forward through the 1st and 2nd AB beads added in this Round at the first repeat of (a).

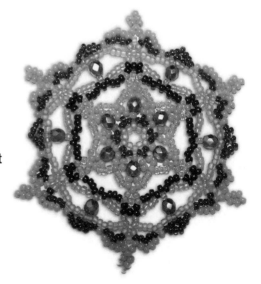

This Round is worked clockwise

Round 6

a) Pick up 5W, go with thread down through the 4th AB bead, R5(a).

b) Pick up 4W, go with thread left to right through the 4th AB bead, R5(b).

c) Pick up 1W, go with thread left to right through the 6th AB bead, R5(b).

d) Pick up 4W, go with thread up through the 2nd AB bead, next repeat right, R5(a).

e) Continue R6 by repeating (a, b, c, d) around 5 more times.

f) With working thread continue forward through the 1st, 2nd, and 3rd W beads added in this Round at the first repeat of (a).

This Round is worked clockwise

Round 7

a) Pick up 3W, go with thread left to right through the 3rd and 4th W beads, R6(a).

b) Pick up 8W, 1C, go with thread through the 1 W bead, R6(c), up through the 1 C bead, and left to right through the 8th W bead just added in this step.

c) Pick up 7W, go with thread left to right through the 2nd and 3rd W beads, next repeat right, R6(a).

d) Continue R7 by repeating (a, b, c) around 5 more times.

e) With working thread continue forward through the 1st W bead added in this Round at the first repeat of (a).

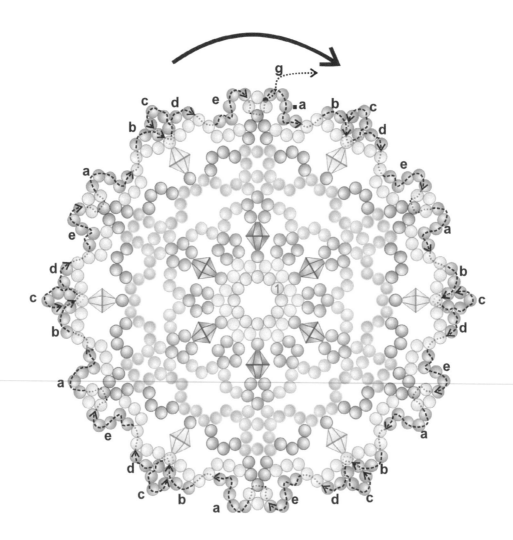

This Round is worked clockwise

Round 8

a) Pick up 5W, go with thread left to right through the 4th and 5th W beads, R7(b).

b) Pick up 3W, go with thread left to right through the 8th W bead, R7(b).

c) Pick up 4W, go with thread left to right through the 3rd W bead added in this Round at (b), the 8th W bead, R7(b), and the 1st W bead just added in this step.

d) Pick up 2W, go with thread left to right through the 3rd and 4th W beads, R7(c).

e) Pick up 5W, go with thread down through the 3 W beads, R7(a), left to right through the 3rd W bead, R6(a), and up through the 1st W bead, R7(a).

f) Continue R8 by repeating (a, b, c, d, e) around 5 more times.

g) With working thread continue forward through the 1st W bead added in this Round at the first repeat of (a).

This Round is worked clockwise

Round 9

a) Pick up 8W, go with thread down through the 3rd W bead just added in this step.

b) Pick up 2W, go with thread down through the 5th W bead, R8(e), the 3rd W bead, R7(a), left to right through the 3rd W bead, R6(a), up through the 1st W bead, R7(a), the 1st W bead, R8(a), and the 1st W bead added in this Round at (a).

c) Pick up 4W, go with thread left to right through the 5th W bead, R8(a).

d) Pick up 1W, go with thread left to right through the 1st and 2nd W beads, R8(b), the 4th, 3rd, 2nd W beads, R8(c), and the 2 W beads, R8(d).

e) Pick up 1W, go with thread left to right through the 1st W beads, R8(e).

f) Pick up 5W, go with thread left to right through the 5th W bead, R8(a), the 3rd W bead, R7(a), left to right through the 3rd W bead, R6(a), up through the 1st W bead, R7(a), and the 1st W bead, R8(a).

g) Pick up 8W, go with thread down through the 3rd W bead just added in this step.

h) Pick up 1W, go with thread down through the 5th W bead added in this Round at (f), left to right through the 5th W bead, R8(e), the 3rd W bead, R7(a), left to right through the 3rd W bead, R6(a), up through the 1st W bead, R7(a), the 1st W bead, R8(a), and up through the 1st W bead added in this Round at (g).

i) Continue R9 by repeating (c, d, e, f, g, h) around 4 more times. Repeat (c, d, e) 1 time.

j) Pick up 4W, go with thread down through the 2nd W bead added in this Round at (b).

Weave the working thread into the snowflake and end.

Snowflake Ornament #13
2-1/8 Inches

W = Miyuki® 11/0 seed bead, #528, all Rounds
C = 4mm crystal AB, R4

W = Miyuki® 11/0 seed bead, #284, R1, 2, 4, 6
      Miyuki® 11/0 seed bead, #366, R3, 5
C = 4mm crystal, light pink, R4

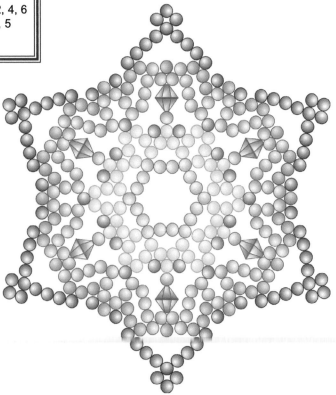

Bead Counts by Rounds
R1 - 18 seeds
R2 - 54 seeds
R3 - 18 seeds
R4 - 102 seeds, 6 crystal
R5 - 48 seeds
R6 - 84 seeds

Round 1
Pick up 18W, make a circle and go with thread through the 1st W bead just added. Continue with working thread around through all 18 beads again, plus go through the 1st bead again. Circle of 18 made, (C18).

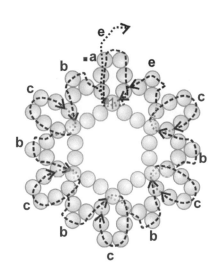

Round 2
a) Pick up 6W, go with thread forward through 1 W bead in C18, same bead that the working thread is exiting, and the 1st W bead just added in this step.
b) Pick up 4W, skip over 2 W beads and go with working thread through the next 1 W bead in C18 as shown.
c) Pick up 5W, go with thread down through the 4th W bead, added in this Round at (b), 1 W bead in C18, and forward through the 1st W bead just added in this step.
d) Continue R2 by repeating (b, c), around 4 more times.
e) Pick up 3W, go with thread down through the 6th W bead added in this Round at (a), forward through 1 W bead in C18, and the 1st, 2nd and 3rd W beads added in this Round at (a).

This Round is worked clockwise
Round 3
a) Pick up 1W, go with thread down through the 4th and 5th W beads, R2(a or c).
b) Pick up 1W, go with thread left to right through the 2nd W bead, R2(b or e).
c) Pick up 1W, go with thread up through the 2nd and 3rd W beads, R2(a or c).
d) Continue R3 by repeating (a, b & c) around 5 more times.
e) Continue with working thread forward through the 1 W bead in the first repeat of (a) this Round.

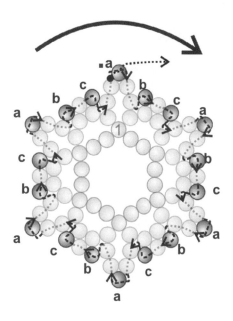

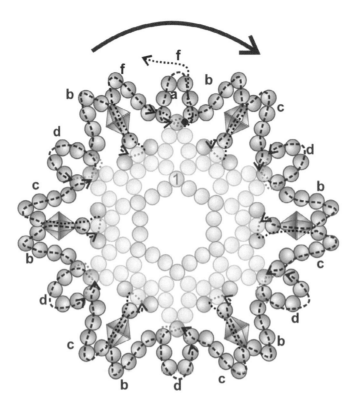

Round 4

a) Pick up 6W, go with thread left to right through 1 W bead, R3(a), and the 1st W bead just added in this step.

b) Pick up 5W, 1C, 1W, go with thread left to right through the 2nd W bead, R2(b or e), and up through the last W and 1 C beads just added in this step.

c) Pick up 6W, go with thread left to right through the 1 W bead, R3(a).

d) Pick up 5W, go with thread down through the 6th W bead added in this Round at (c), 1 W bead, R3(a), and forward through the 1st W bead just added in this step.

e) Continue R4 by repeating (b, c, d) around 4 more times. Repeat (b) 1 time.

f) Pick up 5W, go with thread down through the 6th W bead added in this Round at (a), left to right through 1 W bead, R3(a), and up through the 1st, 2nd and 3rd W beads added in this Round at (a).

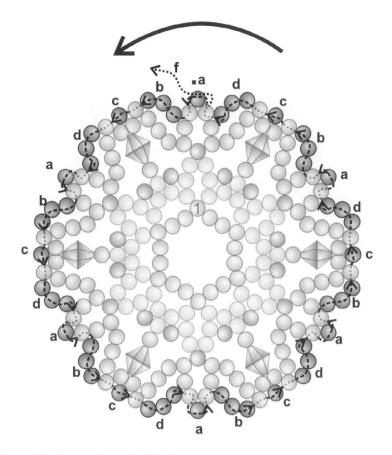

This Round is worked counter-clockwise

Round 5

a) Pick up 1W, go with thread down through the 4th W bead R4(a or d).

b) Pick up 3W, go with thread right to left through the 2nd W bead, R4(c or f).

c) Pick up 1W, go with thread right to left through the 4th W bead, R4(b).

d) Pick up 3W, go with thread up through the 3rd W bead, R4(d or a).

e) Continue R5 by repeating (a, b, c, d) around 5 more times.

f) Continue with working thread forward through the 1W bead in the first repeat of (a) this Round.

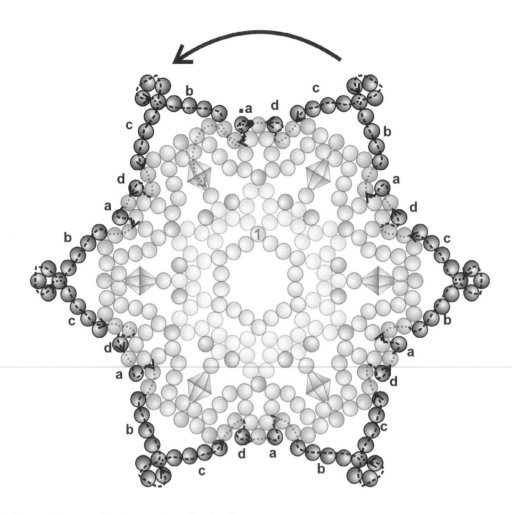

Round 6

a) Pick up 1W, go with thread right to left through the 1st and 2nd W beads, R5(b).

b) Pick up 8W, go with thread down through the 5th W bead just added in this step.

c) Pick up 4W, go with thread right to left through the 2nd and 3rd W beads, R5(d).

d) Pick up 1W, go with thread right to left through the 1 W bead, R5(a).

f) Continue R6 by repeating (a, b, c, d) around 5 more times.

d) Weave the working thread into the snowflake and end.

SNOWFLAKE ORNAMENT #14
2 INCHES

W = Miyuki® 11/0 seed bead, #1920, R1, 3, 5
AB = Miyuki® 11/0 seed bead, #250, R2, 4
U = 3mm Miyuki® cube beads, crystal , R1

W = Miyuki® 11/0 seed bead, #25F, R1, 3, 5
AB = Miyuki® 11/0 seed bead, #591, R2, 4
U = 3mm Miyuki® cube beads, #149, R1

Bead Counts by Rounds
R1 - 96 seeds, 6 - 3mm cubes
R2 - 54 seeds
R3 - 66 seeds
R4 - 90 seeds
R5 - 78 seeds

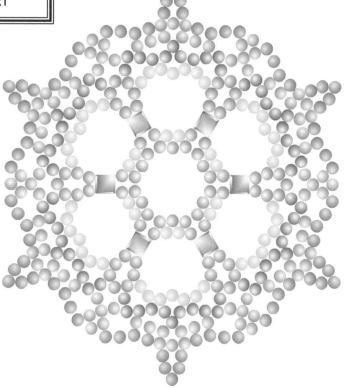

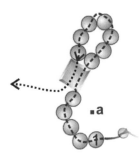

Round 1

a) Pick up 5W, 1U, 7W, go with thread down through the 1 U bead just added in this step.
b) Continue R1 by repeating (a) around 5 more times.
c) With working thread continue forward through the first 5 W, 1 U, 7th and 6th W beads, this Round at the first repeat of (a), as shown.

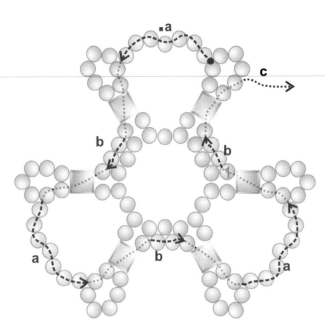

Round 2, part 1

a) Pick up 7AB, go with thread down through the 1st and 2nd W beads (of the 7W), 1 U bead, in the next repeat left R1(a), and the 1st W bead (of the 5W) in the next repeat left, R1(a).
b) Pick up 2AB, go with thread up through the 5th W bead (of the 5W), R1(a), and the 1 U, 7th and 6th W or the 1st and 2nd W, (of the 7W) beads in the next repeat left, R1(a).
c) Continue by repeating (a, b) around 2 more times. Please follow diagram for clarity.

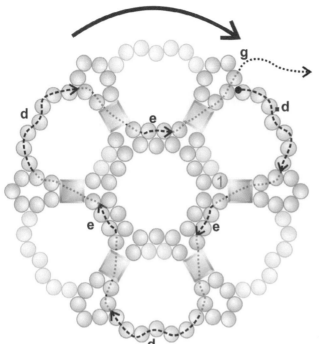

Round 2, part 2

d) Pick up 7AB, go with thread down through the 6th and 7th W beads (of the 7W), 1 U bead, in the next repeat left R1(a), and the 5th W bead (of the 5W) in the next repeat right, R1(a).

e) Pick up 2AB, go with thread up through the 1st W bead (of the 5W), R1(a), and the 1 U, 1st and 2nd W beads (of the 7W) in the next repeat right, R1(a).

f) Continue by repeating (d, e) around 2 more times.

g) With working thread continue forward through the 1 U, 1st, 2nd and 3rd W beads (of the 7W), added in R1(a), as shown.

Round 3

a) Pick up 4W, skip over 2 AB and go with thread left to right through the next 1 AB bead, R2(d or a).

b) Pick up 3W, skip over 1 AB, go with thread left to right through the next 1 AB bead, R2(d or a).

c) Pick up 4W, go with thread down through the 5th, 6th, 7th W beads and up through the 1st, 2nd, 3rd W beads, R1(a), as shown.

d) Continue R3 by repeating (a, b, c) around 5 more times.

e) With working thread continue forward through the 1st and 2nd W beads, added in this Round at the first repeat of (a).

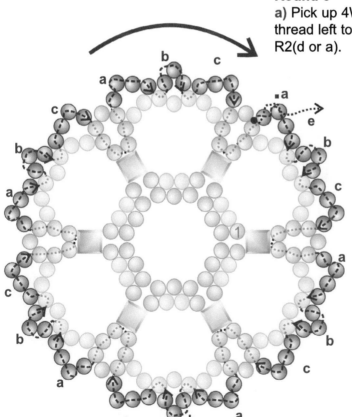

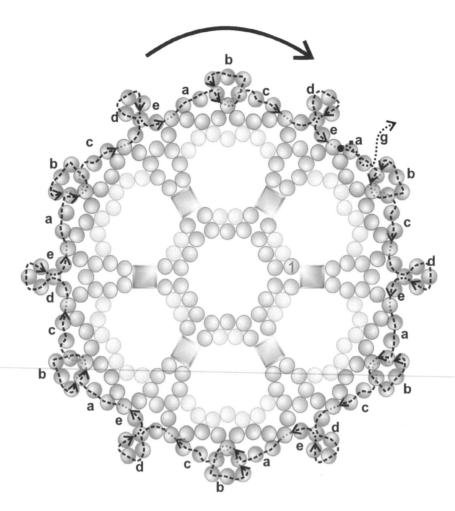

Round 4

a) Pick up 3AB, go with thread left to right through the 2nd W bead, R3(b).

b) Pick up 4AB, go with thread left to right through the 3rd AB bead, this Round at (a), the 2nd W bead, R3(b), and the 1st AB bead just added in this step.

c) Pick up 2AB, go with thread left to right through the 3rd W bead, R3(c).

d) Pick up 5AB, go with thread down through the 2nd AB bead just added in this step.

e) Pick up 1AB, go with thread left to right through the 2nd W bead, R3(a).

f) Continue R4 by repeating (a, b, c, d, e) around 5 more times.

g) With working thread continue forward through the 1st and 2nd AB beads added in this Round at the first repeat of (a).

Round 5

a) Pick up 1W, go with thread up through the 4th AB bead, R4(b).

b) Pick up 5W, go with thread down through the 2nd AB bead, R4(b).

c) Pick up 1W, go with thread left to right through the 1st AB bead, R4(c).

d) Pick up 3W, go with thread down through the 3rd AB bead and up through the 5th AB bead, R4(d).

e) Pick up 3W, go with thread left to right through the 2nd AB bead, R4(a).

f) Continue R5 by repeating (a, b, c, d, e) around 5 more times.

g) Weave the working thread into the snowflake and end.

2913400R00044

Printed in Great Britain
by Amazon.co.uk, Ltd.,
Marston Gate.